The Villages and Rural Life
of
WEST CHESHIRE

A Portrait in Old Picture Postcards

by

Andrew Jenkins

S.B. Publications
1991

For my daughter, Kate Louise, who was born on 10 July 1991, whilst this book was being written.

First published in 1991 by S.B. Publications,
Unit 2, The Old Station Yard, Pipe Gate,
Market Drayton, Shropshire, TF9 4HY

ISBN 1 85770 005 8

Typeset, printed and bound by Manchester Free Press,
Paragon Mill, Jersey St., Manchester, M4 6FP. Tel: 061-236 8822

CONTENTS

S.B. Publications

Front Cover: Tarvin Church and Church Cottages — A postcard illustrated by Alfred Robert Quinton (1853-1934), one of the most prolific postcard artists, who travelled extensively throughout the British Isles by bicycle, making sketches and watercolour illustrations for use on postcards.

INTRODUCTION

About This Book

Early picture postcards are now regarded as historical documents giving a unique portrait of everyday life at the turn of the century. After years of neglect in attics and old albums they have now been rediscovered and are eagerly collected. The postcards illustrated in this book have been selected from my collection which I started nearly fifteen years ago. They portray the villages and rural life in my home county of Cheshire. The area covered by the illustrations is roughly east of the Wirral and west of the M6 motorway and they have been arranged in the form of a journey from Runcorn in the north to Audlem in the south. I have chosen the postcards to give a broad picture of rural life in the county, therefore some villages and common views have had to be omitted.

For many older residents of Cheshire the illustrations will bring back pleasant memories, whilst for others the book will form a useful guide to some of the lesser-known sights of the area. It is also hoped that the growing band of local historians and postcard collectors will find this material of interest. In some cases these postcards are the only record of the people and events depicted and are therefore worthy of further study.

Postcards of Cheshire

By present standards early postcards covered an enormous range of views, subjects and events. This can be explained by looking at the development of the picture postcard at the end of the nineteenth century.

The plain postcard was invented in Austria in 1869, and by 1894 picture cards had been permitted, causing their popularity to increase rapidly. Photographic reproduction in newspapers was poor and there were no radios or telephones. An efficient Post Office could guarantee next day delivery, so picture postcards became an ideal method of transmitting news and pictorial information. A postcard collecting craze developed; in 1907 over two million were sent every day in Britain. Almost every village would have a postcard photographer producing views and covering local events. Often the cards would be published within hours of the event taking place. Photography was still in its infancy and the equipment cumbersome, making the visit of the postcard photographer quite an event. Curious locals, especially children, would gather to watch, and these groups have sometimes been captured on the views produced.

Hand-coloured and artistic cards were also available. The wife of the Chester publisher Thos. Swift travelled with the photographer, making watercolour sketches of the places visited. These would then be given to outworkers, who used them as masters for the colouring of the production run of postcards which was again done with watercolours. The cards were put on sale at '1d plain, 2d coloured'.

After 1908 the development of the cinema and telephone led to a decline in postcard sending. There was a short respite during World War I but the golden age of postcards was now over.

Rural Cheshire

Cheshire is a county rich in contrasts, comprising parts of the Welsh hills to the west and the Pennines to the east with the fertile Cheshire plain between. It has long been an important communication corridor, especially in recent years, with the growth of industry in south Lancashire and the Potteries.

This book covers the mid-Cheshire sandstone ridge and the Cheshire plain, an area noted for its prosperous dairy farms and 'magpie architecture' — traditional half-timbered black and white buildings. For many hundreds of years it has also been the home of wealthy landowners, and large areas of the countryside were dominated by the mansions and estates of the great Cheshire families. Many villages were developed for these estates and often retain a distinctive appearance such as at Aldford, Great Budworth and Harthill. In the nineteenth century rich industrialists from neighbouring areas continued this tradition, building country houses or hunting residences in the county. With the exception of the salt district around Northwich and Middlewich the industrial revolution has left few scars on the area. In recent times, with the decline in agricultural work, the villages have provided homes for people working in the towns, and rural life has become less self-sufficient. Despite modern pressures for development, many villages retain their rural atmosphere. The main cause of change in recent years has been the increasing use of motor vehicles, which have turned quiet lanes into busy highways and filled empty village streets.

Hopefully this book will emphasise the need to preserve the rural landscape of Cheshire for future generations.

THE COAT OF ARMS OF CHESHIRE, 1905

Most English counties and towns were included in this extensive series of heraldic postcards published by Stoddart & Co., in 1905. The arms of Cheshire are based on those of the Earl of Chester and feature three garbs (golden wheatsheaves) on a blue background. This is an appropriate device as the county was once famed for its cereal farms and was described as 'the breadbasket of England'. The motto is translated as 'The ancients look after the ancient of days'.

COUNTY OF CHESHIRE.

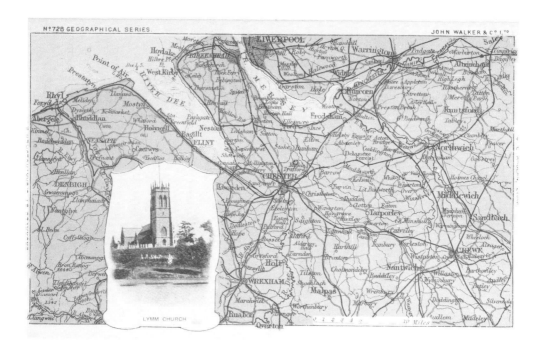

LYMM CHURCH

MAP OF WEST CHESHIRE, c. 1904

This is one of a series of several hundred map postcards covering the whole country. They were published by John Walker & Co. in 1904 at the height of the postcard collecting craze. Each card carried an inset picture of a local view. The map will help to locate many of the places described in the following pages.

HALTON CASTLE, RUNCORN, 1905
At the time this photograph was taken Halton village had a population of just over one thousand. However in the last twenty-five years the fields shown here have disappeared under the houses and shopping centre of Runcorn New Town. The postcard depicts the castle built in the thirteenth century on its sandstone outcrop. It was remodelled by James Wyatt in the 1770s to improve the view from Norton Priory. Notice the advertisement for the Castle Hotel on the walls. To the right is the church of St Mary, and the original village street can be seen running along the base of the castle mound.

SUTTON WEAVER STATION, c.1910

On the outskirts of Runcorn New Town and almost surrounded by the M56 motorway Sutton Weaver was once a quiet rural community. However proximity to the Liverpool to Crewe and Warrington to Chester railway lines meant that the village was provided with two stations. This view is on the former line built by the London and North Western Railway. The station staff and track repair gang pose on the tracks for the photographer, unperturbed by the approaching express. Both the stations have now closed; this one was an early casualty of a decline in passengers and shut in November 1931. Ironically had it survived it would now be ideally situated for the new town.

PEAR TREE FARM. ACTON.   DESTROYED BY FIRE

FIRE AT PEAR TREE FARM, ACTON BRIDGE, 1908

Unfortunately no details can be traced of this fire at Acton Bridge, near Weaverham. The postcard is, however, of interest, as the farm building appears to have been of a longhouse type construction. Longhouses or cross-passage houses date from early medieval times and very few exist today. The building provided accommodation for the farmer and his animals under the same roof. Here the farmers living quarters were in the front portion of the building with the cow-shed or shippon behind. A cross-passage, the door to which can be seen behind the barrel, separated animals and humans.

The Swing Bridge — Acton, Cheshire

RIVER WEAVER, ACTON BRIDGE, 1912

A view of the old swing bridge over the River Weaver at Acton Bridge. The river was canalised in the eighteenth century which enabled sea-going vessels to reach the salt-producing district around Northwich and Winsford. In 1932 a new bridge, the first in this country to rest on a floating pontoon, was built a few hundred yards downstream and this bridge was removed. The abutments can still be seen in the garden of the Leigh Arms, shown in the background. The house on the left has also been demolished. Note the three men who were employed to maintain and operate the bridge.

High Street, Weaverham.

WEAVERHAM HIGH STREET, 1904

The village has seen many changes since the abbot of Vale Royal Abbey built a prison and court house here; now it is virtually a suburb of Northwich. However when this postcard was produced Weaverham was described as 'a quaint country town'. The eastern end of the old High Street is shown here with Smiths Lane on the left. Most of the buildings are still standing, including the Wheatsheaf public house in the centre of the picture. The cottage to the right is now a bank. A large group of children can be seen playing in the street, including two who are dangerously hitching a ride on the back of the cart belonging to Winnington Co-operative Society.

MARBURY HALL AND MERE, NEAR NORTHWICH, 1912

There has been a hall on this site overlooking Budworth mere since the middle ages. The Barry family inherited the estate in the eighteenth century and in 1856 the architect Salvin was commissioned to enlarge the house into a vast imitation of a French chateau, with pavilion roofs and French style dormer windows. Marbury Hall was sold in the 1930s and became a country club. It was taken over by the army in World War II, and subsequently I.C.I. used the site as offices.

The house was demolished in 1969 and the grounds are now a country park.

Great Budworth, Cheshire (Copyright)

GREAT BUDWORTH VILLAGE, 1906

This is one of the most picturesque villages in the county, built on a low hill overlooking Budworth mere. It possesses many fine seventeenth-century timber-framed cottages with an interesting variety of chimney designs, some of which can be seen here. The village has close associations with nearby Arley Hall estate; many of the buildings were renovated by the Egerton-Warburton family in the nineteenth century. This view depicts the village square opposite the fifteenth-century church. The unusual wrought iron sign belongs to the George and Dragon Inn, designed in 1875 by John Douglas, a renowned Cheshire architect. Note the little girl with brush and pail collecting manure for the garden.

The village of Big Budworth! you may travel England round,
There is not such a village in the kingdom to be found,
It signifies in Saxon "by the water an abode."
And still that water floweth as in olden time it flow'd.

So pure so bright, both day and night it bubbles and it flows,
The Running Pump they call it there, as everybody knows;
But, mind ye, 'tis the water that is running, not the pump—
'Tis all the pump can do to stand upon its rotten stump.

His sweetheart there the lover meets and tells her not to doubt,
His love shall last so long as runs that water from the spout,
And there old crones together flock when summer evenings close,
And faster than the Running Pump the village gossip flows.

In every sky there is a cloud, however bright the morn,
In every sweet a bitter, and in every rose a thorn;
So one fine day that fountain sweet sent forth a bitter smell,
Each lass who held her can there had to hold her nose as well.

How this befell tho' none could tell, yet one and all declare
Their thirst to quench with such a stench was more than they could bear;
Each school miss wrote to tell mama their tea they could not take,
The more they fill the teapot, still the more their stomachs ache.

Of yore, if this had happen'd, they'd have sworn some wicked witch
Hi d'dipp'd her broom and stirr'd it up with brimstone and with pitch;
That hag the doom of witchcraft had been fated to endure,
They'd have burnt her into ashes to effect a water cure.

Some laid the blame on Willett, he, who doctors all the town,
The physic, which his patients could not swallow, had pour'd down;
Some said it was a trick which Wright the publican had play'd,
That the water he had focussed for the good of his own trade.

The master of the school he said it tasted of red ink:
Said Newhall, 'tis the overflow of cesspool or of sink:
John Lewis, when they told him, flatly said it was not true,
They went and told the Steward, but he only said "pooh! pooh."

They resolv'd to hold a Meeting, and they call'd it then and there;
Drinkwater was the proper man they said to take the chair;
They borrow'd paper, pen and ink, and straightway they began
To write a requisition to the Squire, and thus it ran:

"We, the undersign'd inhabitants of Budworth, Budworth Big,
Potatoes now we cannot boil, we cannot scald a pig;
And those who send their milk away to Warrington for sale,
Have not a drop of water fit to teem into the pail."

THE RUNNING PUMP.

A LEGEND OF BIG BUDWORTH.

By the late R. E. Egerton-Warburton.

"Should the Vicar bring an action you will have to pay the shot
If you stint us in cold water you will find yourself in hot;
This petition, its condition showeth plainly by the dirt
That we cannot wash our fingers, no—nor change our Sunday shirt.

"The water, like the pump itself, quite rotten is and stale,
Of that bereft we've nothing left but George and Dragon ale:
We cannot mix our porridge with no water in the pot;
If we do not die of hunger we shall perish of dry rot."

"Our faith upon the Running Pump has hitherto been pinn'd,
But how when short of water can we hope to raise the wind;
So Squire, unless we get redress, and pretty quickly too,
We, your tenants of Big Budworth we will wash our hands of you
Cooke, Dutton, Burgess, Barber, Sumner, Bebbington and Platt,
All, young and old, their hands uphold and say "aye! aye!" to that
Then those who cannot write their names a cross upon it scrawl
And straight they went their document to carry to the Hall.

The Squire thought first the Fenians had from prison broke away,
He look'd again and said, "Good men what come ye here to say!
Has Rinderpest broke out afresh! is Budworth Church on fire!"
"Fire! not a bit! read what we've writ, 'tis water we require."

A notion, as he read it, flash'd like lightning through his mind,
Or salt or sulphur it might be, or both of them combined;
Though the gold mine prov'd a failure, though the nugget was no go,
Still gold into my pocket from the Running Pump may flow.

"I'll draw a plan, and spick and span build up a new hotel;
The world forsaking Harrogate, shall fly to Budworth well,
It may turn out a cure for gout, it may be full of steel,
Weak nerves to cure, which all endure, who call themselves genteel.
"Nay! who can tell, to try this well her majesty the Queen
May condescend to come and spend a summer at the Dene."
He bade his groom go saddle him a hunter of good-speed,
And straight, across the Arley Moss he prick'd his flying steed.

He reached the Pump—alas! when there he found himself at fault
It neither smelt of sulphur, neither tasted it of salt:
The wry face he made o'er it told the thing was past a joke,
That, sure enough, was not the stuff for fashionable folk.

He bade them dig, and spadeful upon spadeful they upcast,
And what do you think of all this stink the reason was at last!
A marvel then no longer how this strange thing came to pass
Some one there had been and gone and buried a dead ass

THE LEGEND OF THE RUNNING PUMP, GREAT BUDWORTH, c.1906

Rowland Eyles Egerton-Warburton was known as the 'Rhyming Poet of Arley Hall'. He was associated with the Tarporley Hunt Club and for many years wrote of its adventures in verse and composed its drinking songs. In 1869 he built a pumphouse for the well at Great Budworth, and wrote this poem which can be seen inscribed above the pump. The verse refers to several local characters of the time, but it is not known if the story has any factual basis! Other verses can be seen on buildings and signposts in the locality, and in the porch of the George and Dragon. The well was used regularly until mains water arrived in 1934.

MOWING HAY NEAR PICKMERE, 1916

Agriculture was still the main source of employment in Cheshire when this postcard was produced. It depicts a horse-drawn mowing machine cutting grass for haymaking. The peaceful scene belies the arduous working conditions endured by farm labourers at the turn of the century. In June, when mowing coincided with lifting the early potato crop, the working day often lasted from 3am until 8pm with a break at noon for 'baggings'; a meal of bread, cheese and beer. The horse-mower was a relatively new invention at this time; many farms still used hand scythes for cutting hay.

SUMMERTIME HAYMAKING IN A PICKMERE MEADOW
SHOWING BUDWORTH IN THE DISTANCE

HAYMAKING NEAR GREAT BUDWORTH, c.1910

Another postcard in the series shows a gang of five men using a horse rake to collect the hay into heaps for drying. Using modern machinery this task can now be performed by one person. In the background is the village of Great Budworth dominated by the church of St Mary. Prosperous farming in the fifteenth century brought wealth to the area and encouraged the building of these large churches.

PICKMERE LAKE, c.1912

This busy summer scene was once common along the shores of Pickmere. Large numbers of trippers used to arrive either in horse-drawn waggons or by train to Lostock station. They would then walk across the fields to the mere. Here there were picnic grounds and boats for sailing or fishing. A funfair was built on the shore, with roundabouts and a helter-skelter. Over 300 wooden chalets were provided for those wishing to stay for a longer period. Local farms and cottages did a brisk trade in teas and lemonade for cyclists. Today the mere is quieter, but it can still be a popular spot on summer weekends.

The Oaktree (Marking centre of Cheshire) — Bostock near Northwich.

The Unique Series.

THE OAKTREE, BOSTOCK GREEN, NEAR DAVENHAM, c.1905

Bostock village, between Northwich and Middlewich, is noted for its picturesque cottages, built for workers on the Bostock Hall estate, home of the France-Hayhurst family. The estate provided many amenities for the village, including a laundry and reading rooms. For hundreds of years an old oak tree on the village green was considered to mark the centre of Cheshire. This was felled in 1887 when it became unsafe. The tree shown on this postcard was planted in its place in 1897, Queen Victoria's Jubilee year, by three generations of the France-Hayhurst family. The tree is still there today, although much larger; otherwise the village has seen little change over the years.

DELAMERE STREET. OVER CHESHIRE.

T.S. R&C

"The Unique Series."

DELAMERE STREET, OVER, 1907

At one time Over was a small market town with its own mayor. However it declined until the nineteenth century, when the salt industry at Winsford brought expansion. Now the towns have merged, Over becoming a suburb of Winsford New Town. This has brought great change to the area, including this view of the Winsford end of Delamere St looking north from near the roundabout. All the cottages on the right have disappeared, a car showroom replacing those nearest the camera. Notice the entrance gate to the Over Brewery. The building on the extreme left is now known as 'Saxons' public house.

VALE ROYAL ABBEY.

VALE ROYAL ABBEY, NEAR WHITEGATE, 1916

This was once the site of the largest Cistercian abbey in England; however, very little of the original building remains. Edward I laid the first stone in 1277, but building was not completed until 1330. Friction between the monks and the local population led to violent uprisings. On one occasion a monk was murdered and a game of football played with his head. Henry VIII expelled the monks in the Dissolution and the estate passed first to the Holcroft then to the Cholmondeley families. The abbey was looted by Cromwell's troops in the Civil War and parts of the present building date from this period. Major alterations took place in the eighteenth and nineteenth centuries. At the time this photograph was taken Vale Royal was the seat of Lord Delamere. After being neglected for some years restoration work has now begun.

THE MONKEY HOUSE, WHITEGATE, 1915

A family in a horse and trap pauses outside this unusual building beside the Whitegate to Hartford road. It was originally a gatehouse on the drive between Vale Royal Park and the New or Petty Pool Park. The drive was closed in the early years of this century after a dispute between Lord Delamere of Vale Royal and the District Council. Recently the Monkey House has been extensively restored.

WHITEGATE VILLAGE, 1906

The village church, from which this photograph was taken, is closely associated with Vale Royal Abbey. It stands opposite a white gate leading to the abbey, which was used by the abbot's tenants and from which the village got its name. This view of the green and part of Church Mews is the site of the annual fête and has changed little over the years. Whitegate is supposed to be the birthplace of the Cheshire prophet Nixon, who lived in the fifteenth century. He foretold many strange happenings, including his own demise 'in poverty surrounded by plenty'. He was locked in a cupboard at the royal court and died from starvation!!

The Cheshire Hounds Meet at the Blue Cap Sandiway

THE BLUE CAP INN, SANDIWAY, c.1906

This inn, named after a famous local foxhound, stands beside the Chester to Northwich road at Sandiway. Its hunting associations are aptly shown in this view of people arriving by horse and trap for the start of the hunt. In 1762 Blue Cap won 500 guineas for his master, John Smith Barry, in a race at Newmarket against rival dogs owned by Hugo Meynell. The stakes were so high that much trouble was taken to bring the dogs to perfection. Blue Cap was fed on oatmeal, milk and sheep's trotters, whilst Meynell's dogs were given legs of mutton. The race of 4 miles was won in 8 minutes, an average speed of 30 miles per hour. Blue Cap died in 1772 and is buried in a field nearby.

OAKMERE TOLL BAR, c.1910

This view of the toll house at the junction of the Chester to Manchester Turnpike road (A556) and Tarporley to Warrington road is difficult to recognise today. The site of the toll house is now a large petrol station and the woodland on the right has disappeared due to road widening. Turnpike trusts began in 1663; the tolls collected were used to pay for road improvements. They were most extensive in the eighteenth-century coaching age. By 1864 the Trusts were dissolved, the cost of road repairs falling upon local rates. According to the sign over the door, this toll-house survived by offering accommodation and refreshment to cyclists. Similar toll-houses can still be seen at Kelsall and Mere near Knutsford.

DELAMERE FOREST, c.1912

The present-day forest is but a small remnant of the great forest of Mara and Mondrem which originally extended from the Mersey to Nantwich. It was once the exclusive hunting ground of the Earls of Chester and the Royal Family. The Foresters Court allowed only a privileged few to hunt, collect wood and cultivate the area. By the nineteenth century the court had become a benevolent society, but its officers still held the old titles such as 'Master Forester'. In 1812 a Deafforestation Act reduced the size of the forest considerably, retaining a small area to supply timber for ships in the Napoleonic Wars. Delamere has long been the haunt of gypsies, although the vehicle shown here is more likely to be a horse-drawn touring caravan.

"The Fringe of the Forest" Delamere

PLATELAYERS NEAR DELAMERE STATION, c.1908

A track repair gang at work on the Cheshire Lines Railway near Delamere station. This team of over twenty-five men are replacing worn rails. They are all wearing the traditional 'navvy' uniform of moleskin waistcoats and cloth caps. Note also the complete absence of any mechanical aids. The men on the right are using large metal tongs to lift the rails into position. Many would have left jobs on the land to seek more secure employment on the railways.

THE POST OFFICE AND QUARRY LANE, KELSALL HILL, 1908

The Bronze Age Celts first settled in the area, at Kelsbarrow Castle. Later the Romans built North Watling Street, through the gap in the Cheshire ridge where Kelsall now lies. Kelsall Hill Post Office still stands at the top of the long hill from Tarvin. Most of the staff and local children have assembled to appear on this postcard. Quarry Lane can be seen leading off into the distance. Here there were several freestone quarries providing employment for the villagers. In the 1930s a number of houses were built along the lane, however this view is still easily recognisable.

Kelsall Village, No. 2.

"The Unique Series"

KELSALL VILLAGE, 1905

The village of Kelsall extends down the hill towards Tarvin. At its lower end is the Royal Oak Inn, built around 1900 and shown on the right of this postcard. Nearby is an eighteenth-century gaol, now incorporated into a new house. The thatched cottage on the left has now been replaced by a modern building and in the background the large brick barn has been pulled down. The boy with the bicycle in the centre of the picture is wearing a peaked cap and could be a messenger or delivery boy. On the left hand edge of the road is an early form of child's pushchair.

THE CROSS, TARVIN, 1913

Much of the centre of Tarvin was rebuilt at the end of the eighteenth century, after a disastrous fire in 1752. This is a view of the Cross looking towards Lower Tarvin. The pump was one of three which supplied the village and was the first to be condemned when mains water arrived in the 1920s. Gunnery's grocery store on the left is noteworthy today because the Victorian frontage is still preserved intact. Note the fine display of enamel signs. The building on the right was originally the Bulls Head Inn, but had been converted into The Cross Refreshment Rooms when this photograph was taken.

PROCESSION AT TARVIN, c.1908

This postcard is one of a series recording a procession of ladies and children in their Sunday best outfits through the streets of Tarvin. Possibly this was part of the Wakes Week celebrations. The photograph shows the procession being assembled outside Church Cottages before entering St Andrew's church. Some of the ladies can be seen holding hymn sheets. Church Cottages date from the early sixteenth century and survived the fire in 1752. They have recently been restored.

MEET AT WILLINGTON HALL

JAMES TOMKINSON AT WILLINGTON HALL, 1907

James Tomkinson MP is shown here on horseback in front of Willington Hall, near Kelsall. The hall was built for his father Col. W. Tomkinson by George Latham, in 1829, in the Elizabethan style. It is based on Dorfold Hall near Nantwich, owned by another branch of the family. James Tomkinson was Liberal MP for Crewe from 1900. He was an accomplished horseman and a past-president of Tarporley Hunt Club. On the 10 April 1910, at the age of 70, he was riding in the House of Commons Steeplechase at Epping when tragically he was thrown from his horse at the last fence and killed. Recently Willington Hall was converted into a country hotel, but it is still a meeting place of the Cheshire Hunt.

LIBERAL DEMONSTRATION
WILLINGTON HALL
JUNE.7.06

LIBERAL PARTY RALLY, WILLINGTON HALL, 7 June 1906
In 1906 Joseph Chamberlain's tariff reform policies had split the Conservative government. This led to a landslide victory for the Liberals in the January General Election. On 7 June a demonstration to celebrate local Liberal victories was held at Willington Hall. A large crowd, some of whom are shown here, gathered in the gardens to hear speeches from MPs A.L. Stanley and James Tomkinson. Teas were provided in a large marquee, and musical entertainment was provided by the Winsford Temperance Band. A stirring message was sent to the gathering from the Prime Minister, Henry Campbell Bannerman; "Delighted to hear of your rejoicings over local victories, keep your men disciplined and your weapons bright. Let the memory of the past nerve you for the future."

Post Office, Duddon.

DUDDON POST OFFICE, NEAR TARVIN, c.1910

The local post office used to be one of the centres of rural life and was often combined with the village store. This is the original post office at Duddon, near Tarvin, which was situated at the corner of Back Lane. Before 1920 this half-timbered building was demolished and the post office moved to its present position on the Tarporley side of the Headless Woman Inn, the stables of which can just be seen in the background. The site of the old post office is now a garden. Note the newspaper billboards; one headline proclaims 'Farmworkers Strike in Cheshire'.

'THE HEADLESS WOMAN', DUDDON, NEAR TARVIN, 1916

As the name suggests, this inn commemorates a local ghost. A legend tells of Grace Trigg, a maid at Hockenhull Hall, near Tarvin, who refused to hand over her mistress's jewellery to Cromwell's soldiers. As a result they beheaded her, but she walked with her head tucked under her arm through a tunnel to Duddon, where her ghost can be seen walking the lanes. For many years the inn had a collection of curios, and a headless ship's figurehead in the garden, but this has now disappeared. The building itself has changed little over the years, but the rural atmosphere of this scene has been lost due to road widening.

CHURCH and SCHOOL, HUXLEY.

HUXLEY VILLAGE, c.1910

A farm cart loaded with sacks of grain makes its way through the village, probably to one of the watermills on the River Gowy. Situated between Tattenhall and Tarporley, Huxley is still a quiet place today, and little has changed in this view of the school and St Andrew's church. However, in the past the village was noted as a centre of non-conformist religion. In 1842 eight hundred people attended the celebrations to mark the opening of the New Connection chapel in the centre of the village. This building still exists, but has now been converted into a private house.

UTKINTON HALL, NEAR TARPORLEY, 1907

This was the home of the Done family from around 1240, when Henry Done received the title of Master Forester of Delamere. The symbolic horn is still held by a branch of the family. The hall has seen many changes over the years. The present building, a quarter of its original size, dates from the seventeenth century, when it was rebuilt after an attack by the Royalists. However, it retains many earlier features, such as a massive octagonal oak pillar which may come from the original thirteenth-century house. Other parts of the hall were removed to Tarporley; the sundial to St Helen's church, and the oak staircase to the old Rectory. For the last hundred years Utkinton Hall has served as a dairy farm.

HIGH STREET, TARPORLEY, 1905

The history of Tarporley can be traced back to Saxon times. By 1297 it was known as a borough and had a mayor and a market. The long wide High Street developed in the eighteenth century, when the village was an important stop on the Chester to London coaching route. This quiet scene is of the northern end of the High Street looking towards the Swan Hotel in the distance. The building on the right, now a bank, was once a courthouse complete with dungeon. The cottages to its left have been demolished and a service station erected in their place. The large chestnut tree, now a feature of the village, can be seen in its younger days just to the left of the white cottage.

GARDEN PARTY PROCESSION, TARPORLEY, 1907

A photograph, taken from the steps of the Swan Hotel, of a procession on its way to the garden party which was held each August in the grounds of Tarporley vicarage. Behind the brass band is the Tarporley Fire Brigade on their horse-drawn engine. This was the first voluntary fire brigade in the country, founded by the Earl of Haddington in 1869. On the right, at the corner of Victoria Street, now known as Park Road, is Cluett's Private Hotel, now also renamed the Park Hotel. To its left is the gateway of the Methodist Chapel built in 1868. It was demolished about ten years ago and shops now occupy the site.

THE SWAN HOTEL, TARPORLEY, 1912

This old coaching inn is known throughout Cheshire as the headquarters of the Tarporley Hunt Club. The facade of the hotel was built on to an earlier building in 1769. To the right is the Market House built in 1711, incorporating materials from Utkinton Hall (see p32). The upper floor houses the meeting room of the Hunt Club. Nine gentlemen formed the club in November 1762 to 'enjoy the pleasures of the chase'. Membership gradually increased to include most of the great landowners in the county, and its activities expanded to include racing and a horse show. Members still observe the rules and traditions of the club including its own uniform.

To learn the fashion of the day call at 55 HIGH STREET.

Manor House.

HENRY DUTTON, Draper and Outfitter, Tarporley.

MANOR HOUSE, TARPORLEY, c.1906

An advertising postcard given away by the drapers, Henry Dutton, who kept a shop in the High Street for many years. The illustration is of Tarporley Manor House, situated in the centre of the village. It was built by Ralph Done in 1586 and was originally half-timbered. However, in the nineteenth century the timbering became unsafe and the building was covered in stucco. The gable has now been restored to its original condition. A large beam extends the length of the upper storey, and on this is the inscription; 'Ralph Done Esquyer, the Lorde of thys place' 'Was an eade to thys buldyng in every case'.

36

OLD COTTAGES, HIGH STREET, TARPORLEY, c.1910

A group of local people take an interest in the photographer outside the thatched sandstone cottages which once stood opposite the Manor House on the High Street. The nearest cottage was used as a tea room. They were demolished in the 1940s and replaced by bungalows set back from the road. Compare the size of the telegraph poles with those on page 33. As more lines were added their size increased and they became an eyesore. On some postcards of the village they have been carefully retouched out of the picture. Eventually the cables were placed underground and the poles were removed.

HIGH STREET AND NANTWICH ROAD, TARPORLEY, 1910

A rather bleak view of the Nantwich end of Tarporley High Street, near the Eaton and Birch Heath roads. This area has altered considerably over the years. The shops, including Morgan's grocers on the right, now form part of the Foresters Arms, and the adjacent houses were demolished to form the car park. A lodging house for vagrants existed here in the 1920s. The house on the left has been replaced by a garage forecourt and the land in the background was used for housing in the 1930s. Note the poor state of the road and the cobbled pavements. The joints of meat hanging outside the butcher's shop look particularly unhealthy, exposed to the rain and mud.

THE GENERAL ELECTION, TARPORLEY, 19 January 1910

A rare postcard depicting the supporters of the Hon. Arthur Lyulph Stanley, Liberal MP for Eddisbury, outside his Tarporley committee rooms on polling day. Mr Stanley was elected in 1906. However, although considered to have a safe seat, he was narrowly defeated in this election by a Mr Barnston, the Conservative candidate. A newspaper report stated that on polling day there was much excitement with little business done in Tarporley. At 7.30pm a large crowd gathered at Mr Stanley's committee rooms. The result was declared at Chester Castle the next day, and many people gathered at Tarporley Post Office to hear the news via the telegraph. A feature of this election was the first use of motor cars to rally support for the candidates.

What the Girls at Tarporley have plenty of.

'SAUCE', TARPORLEY, c.1910
This humorous card was one of a series produced in large numbers without a caption and then overprinted for local retailers. There is no record of what caused the young ladies of Tarporley to earn such a reputation!

TARPORLEY RACES, 1905

Tarporley Steeplechases were a great local event, started in 1775 by the Tarporley Hunt Club and originally held on Crabtree Green, near Delamere. After a couple of moves they found their final home in 1877, near Rode Street on the Chester road. Here the racing was over fences and grew in popularity. The races were attended by large crowds, many of whom arrived by special train at Beeston station, and were conveyed to the course in a variety of horse-drawn vehicles. Many famous horses won at Tarporley including several Grand National winners. The course was the first in the north of England to have a Totaliser. After a break during World War I, racing restarted in 1921. The last race was held on 20 April 1939. During World War II the course was used as a prisoner-of-war camp. It has now reverted to open fields.

PORTAL HOUSE, NEAR TARPORLEY, 1909

This postcard depicts Portal shortly after it was completed in 1905. The house was built on the site of an eighteenth-century lodge and construction took five years. It was designed by W.E. Tower for the Hon. Marshall Brooks and is an idealised version of a sixteenth-century timber-framed mansion. A notable feature is the use of older materials in the building such as sixteenth-century Swiss stained glass and fifteenth-century timbers. A wing of the house was demolished in the 1950s, but the remainder has recently been restored and a golfing centre built in part of the park.

THE TRAM SERVICE, PORTAL, TARPORLEY, 1904

As part of the construction of Portal extensive terraced gardens and parklands were created. This required a considerable amount of earthmoving. Top soil was brought by horse and cart from fields around Tarporley and the materials moved around the site by the horse-powered tramway shown here. This rare postcard was probably produced as an ironic comment on Tarporley's answer to the many tramway networks which were being built in towns at this time.

Portal Red Cross Hospital, Tarporley.

PORTAL RED CROSS HOSPITAL, c.1916

During World War I Tarporley became a Remount Depot with up to two hundred horses stabled around the village. Portal was requisitioned for use as a hospital for soldiers returning from the trenches. This postcard shows some of the hospital staff and patients in the courtyard. Plenty of fresh air and sunshine were considered an important part of convalescence. The wooden shelter in the foreground was built to provide this. It was mounted on a turntable and could be moved to keep the patients facing the sun or out of the wind.

Arderne Hall. Cheshire.

ARDERNE HALL, NEAR TARPORLEY, 1904

This was the seat of Sir George Baille-Hamilton Arden, the 11th Earl of Haddington, and was located between Tarporley and Eaton. Arderne was built in the Victorian Gothic style in 1863 on the site of an earlier house, and at one time nearly thirty staff were employed there. It was demolished in 1958, being too large to maintain, and replaced by a smaller building. The garden, however, remains and is noted for its fine trees, including the largest pear tree in Britain. The park has recently been converted into a golf course.

TARPORLEY FLOWER SHOW AND SPORTS, ARDERNE HALL, 1905

A postcard view of the scene at the annual Tarporley Flower Show and Sports which was held as part of the August Wakes week at Arderne Hall park. The flower show was noted for its gooseberry competition for which a special gooseberry gauge was invented by one John Head. The sports included 'flat races for lads and labourers' and a wheelbarrow race. The wakes continued until the outbreak of World War I but were not revived afterwards.

EATON VILLAGE, NEAR TARPORLEY, c.1906

At the turn of the century a visit from the photographer was still a curiosity in many villages, and was guaranteed to attract a group of children, such as those shown here, some of whom appear to be wearing wooden clogs. Eaton is a small agricultural village a couple of miles east of Tarporley. This part of the village on the Cotebrook road was called Little Eaton. The group of sandstone cottages on the right was built into the hillside and known as the Rabbit Borrer (or Burrow). They were demolished in 1955 and replaced by two modern homes. The timber-framed cottage in the background survives, although no longer thatched.

Cote Brook. No. 1.

COTEBROOK VILLAGE, c.1912

Cotebrook, situated north of Tarporley on the Warrington road, used to be known as Utkinton-cum-Rushton, but the name was changed to Cote Brook — the place used for 'coteing' or penning sheep ready for washing. In this view children from the local school, now closed, pose for the photographer. In the background is the nineteenth-century church of St John and the Holy Cross designed by George Edmund Street. Nearby is High Billinge, a hill capped by a clump of trees. It is a noted landmark for miles around and is the last piece of English land to be seen when leaving Liverpool by ship.

Little Budworth

LITTLE BUDWORTH VILLAGE, 1905

The village and its extensive common, a remnant of the forest of Mara and Mondrem, lie between Tarporley and Winsford. Its history is linked with nearby Oulton Hall and the Egerton family. This quiet scene, looking east along the village street, is still recognisable, although there have been some changes. In the left foreground the black and white cottage has disappeared, whilst on the extreme right the old village post office is now a private house. The Red Lion Inn can be seen in the background together with the tower of St Peter's church, built around 1526.

STRAWBERRY PICKERS, NEAR LITTLE BUDWORTH, 1906

Many local people will remember spending their holidays at this back-breaking work. The growing of soft fruit has a long tradition in parts of Cheshire and can still be seen, especially around Kelsall and Farndon. Only the pickers' dress, and the use of wicker baskets instead of cardboard punnets, date the photograph to the early years of this century. Notice the straw laid between the rows of plants to prevent the berries rotting.

Oulton Hall, Oulton Park, near Tarporley

OULTON HALL, LITTLE BUDWORTH, c.1904

The Egerton family were landowners near Oulton Park for nearly five hundred years, and in the reign of Henry VII they became lords of the manor. Their Tudor mansion burnt down in the eighteenth century and was replaced by a house, said to have been designed by Sir John Vanbrugh, which was considerably enlarged and altered in 1826. The park extended over 350 acres and was noted for its herd of over 300 deer. When this postcard was published, Oulton Hall was the home of Sir Philip Egerton, a famous geologist. The house contained a fine art collection, including paintings by Rubens, Van Dyck and Landseer, and statues by Bertolini.

51

The ruins of Oulton Hall after the desastrous fire
Feb 14th 1926

THE FIRE AT OULTON HALL, 14 February 1926

By the 1920s the hall had been leased to an industrialist, Mr F.W. Cooper. At 10.00am on St Valentine's Day 1926 the family was taking breakfast when the housemaid reported that the upper floors were on fire. By 10.30am the Tarporley fire brigade had arrived and about twenty people were in the salon salvaging works of art. Suddenly at 11.30am the roof collapsed, trapping the people below. Two were killed instantly and four died later from their injuries. The fate of the building was sealed and the fire continued to burn for several days. Many valuable paintings, including two Van Dycks and a Landseer, were destroyed. The ruins remained standing until World War II, when they were hit by German bombs. In 1953 the now famous motor racing circuit was built in the park.

CALVELEY

CALVELEY, 1909

The old gentleman in the trilby hat would have difficulty strolling along the middle of the road today. Apart from the increase in traffic on the Chester to Nantwich road (A51) there have been few changes in this view. To the left is the Davenport Arms and in the background is the entrance to Calveley station. This and the nearby Shropshire Union Canal brought industries such as brickmaking and a dairy to the village. There was also a wharf for transferring goods from canal to railway. Now the station and the old industries have gone and the canal no longer carries commercial traffic.

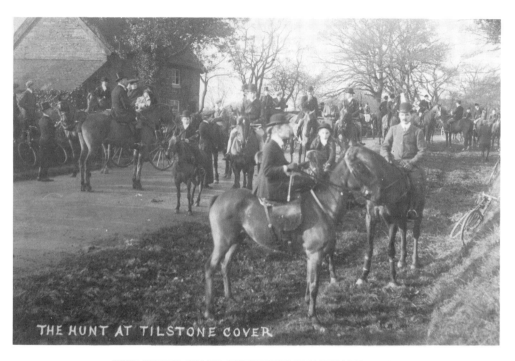

THE HUNT AT TILSTONE COVER

THE HUNT, NEAR TILSTONE FEARNALL, c.1907
A fine view of a meet at Tilstone Fearnall, between Tarporley and Alpraham. The cottage in the background, at the end of the lane to Bunbury, still stands, although much enlarged. Nearby a dip in the main road is known as Haunted Hollow after several people reported seeing there the 10ft-tall ghost of a monk.

'GARDENHURST', NEAR TARPORLEY, c.1906

James Gordon Houghton had Gardenhurst built between Tarporley and Tiverton as a hunting lodge in 1886. However by the 1920s it was empty, being too costly to maintain. During World War II troops were billeted in the house. After the war Gardenhurst was converted into Hampton House preparatory school, which lasted until 1965 when the building was demolished. Five houses were built in the grounds during 1969; however the original entrance lodge is still standing beside the A49.

TIVERTON HILL AND BEESTON BROOK, 1914

A view looking down Tiverton Hill towards the railway and Beeston Auction in the early days of motoring. The road surface has yet to be metalled, hence the cloud of dust put up by the car crossing the canal bridge. The shop on the right was called 'The Farmers Invention' and was owned by E.C. Chamberlain, a well-known local figure who supplied agricultural equipment. At one time he employed seven saddle makers and regularly visited his customers by pony and trap. The shop now sells spares for canal cruisers. In the background much of the woodland was quarried away in the 1960s to provide building sand.

BEESTON CATTLE AUCTION, 1910

The cattle market at Beeston Brook was built beside the Chester to Crewe railway. This was a boon to local farmers who could buy and sell stock from a wide area. In this busy scene a row of railway cattle wagons can be seen in the background. Their sides are white with limewash, used to prevent the spread of disease. The auction was obviously a great attraction for the local schoolboys, who can be seen on and behind the sheep pens. Note the two gentlemen in bowler hats; they are probably auctioneers or cattle dealers. The market is still a focal point for the farming community although all stock movements are now made by road.

EXPRESS PASSING THROUGH
BEESTON CASTLE STATION

BEESTON CASTLE AND TARPORLEY STATION, 1911

The station was built by the Chester and Crewe Railway (later London and North Western Railway) on land provided by Lord Tollemache, and opened in 1840. It served a wide area and had facilities for transporting milk and livestock as well as passengers. Milk churns can be seen on the platform. The train is a non-stop express from North Wales and Chester to Crewe drawn by a LNWR 4-6-0 locomotive. Beeston Castle station was closed completely on 18 April 1966 and has now been demolished.

BEESTON CASTLE AND TARPORLEY STATION FORECOURT, 1908

A busy scene outside the station as a variety of horse-drawn vehicles arrive to meet the train. This was probably a special occasion, such as a race-day at Tarporley Racecourse. Notice the cabs and their drivers wearing top hats. These would have been attached to the large country houses in the district. The station was over two miles from Tarporley, so the London and North Western Railway ran a horse-bus to the village. It was painted in the black and white livery of the railway company and the journey cost 6d. This can be seen waiting behind the lamp-post.

BEESTON TOWERS.

BEESTON TOWERS ('THE WILD BOAR'), 1910

At the top of the hill between Beeston Auction and Bunbury is The Wild Boar Hotel. This was formerly known as Beeston Towers, and was built in 1886 for John Naylor, a timber merchant from Warrington. The Naylor brothers, John and Robert are noteworthy for completing the first recorded walk from Land's End to John O'Groats in 1871, taking nine weeks to complete the journey.

Note the damson trees in blossom; these are a typical feature of the Cheshire countryside.

BUNBURY VILLAGE, 1916

The infant River Gowy divides the village into Higher and Lower Bunbury. The original Saxon settlement was at Higher Bunbury, where the fourteenth-century collegiate church now stands. This postcard shows the centre of Lower Bunbury and includes an interesting collection of houses. On the left is 'Brantwood', built in 1831. The house incorporates the old Bridewell, or lock-up, constructed of sandstone blocks. The black and white cottage opposite dates from the seventeenth century and is one of the oldest in the village. In the nineteenth century the upper floor was used as a schoolroom. A group of schoolboys can be seen in the distance, and an early charabanc is parked outside the cottages.

The Image House, Bunbury, Cheshire
"Clock Abbot" in "The Shiny Night, by Beatrice Tunstall

THE IMAGE HOUSE, NEAR BUNBURY, c.1931

This cottage, which can be found on the Whitchurch road near Bunbury Heath, achieved notoriety in 1931 when it became the subject of *The Shiny Night,* a novel by Beatrice Tunstall. In the book, a poacher who was transported to Australia returned to the village and built the house, including the effigies of his enemies which can be seen on the walls. Another story records that the house was built in a day when, according to tradition, if it could be proved that a squatter could erect a home and have smoke coming from the chimney within one day, the property became his. The images could also have been intended to ward off evil spirits or 'buggins'. The building certainly dates from the early 1800s and was part of the Peckforton Estate.

SPURSTOW SKETH, NEAR BUNBURY, 1908

Spurstow is a scattered community just south of Bunbury. It achieved fame some two hundred years ago due to a mineral spring known as Spurstow White Water, which was claimed to have curative powers. This postcard is something of a curiosity as the district known as Spurstow Sketh does not appear on the map. *The Place Names of Cheshire* records that the name, meaning track or course, was last used in 1840 to describe the area around Whitegates, on the Peckforton road. However this postcard shows that the name 'Sketh' was still known in 1908. Quite why such an elaborate postcard of these cottages should be produced is a mystery. Some of the buildings depicted can still be seen in the area.

Beeston Smithy and the Castle.

BEESTON VILLAGE AND CASTLE, c.1906

Beeston is a scattered village of about 300 people and is dominated by the castle on its rocky crag. Many of the farms and houses were owned by the Tollemache family. In this view the castle can be seen overlooking the village to the right. The timber-framed house advertises teas for visitors to the castle. The building in the right foreground is Beeston smithy, which is still operating as a garage and agricultural engineer.

THE WELL, BEESTON CASTLE, c.1910

A party of Edwardian tourists rest after the 300ft climb to the top of Beeston Castle hill. The climb must have been difficult for the ladies in those hats and long skirts. The castle was built in 1225 by Ranulf Blundeville, Earl of Chester, as part of the Welsh border defences, and was virtually impregnable on its cliff top site. It was partially destroyed by the Parliamentarians in the Civil War, after several sieges. The roofed building covers the well, which is over 370ft deep. Richard II is thought to have hidden a vast treasure at the foot of the well, but, despite repeated attempts, the buried fortune has never been found.

CYCLONE AT
PECKFORTON.
OCT 27 1913   NO.1

THE PECKFORTON CYCLONE, 27 October 1913

On the evening of 27 October 1913, Cheshire and south Lancashire were hit by a severe cyclonic storm which brought devastation to a wide area. One person was killed and many injured. A narrow band of country between Malpas and Widnes was affected by a tornado-like wind accompanied by torrential rain and thunder. The wind uprooted trees and damaged buildings in its path. Greenhouses at Peckforton Castle were destroyed and the roof was torn off Castle Gate Farm at Beeston. This view of the damage along the Beeston road at Peckforton is one of a series of twelve illustrating the aftermath of the storm, and was published shortly after the event.

THE 'ELEPHANT AND CASTLE', PECKFORTON, c.1910

This unusual statue can be seen in the garden of a cottage in Peckforton village. It was carved from a block of sandstone by John Watson, a stonemason, in 1859. It is said to be modelled on the coat of arms of the Corbett family, former landowners in the area. Mr Watson was obviously quite a character. He was employed in the building of the Grosvenor Bridge in Chester and he used to walk the fifteen miles to and from Peckforton every day. In his spare time he worked on the Elephant and Castle. His work can also be seen on nearby Peckforton Castle. The statue is currently being restored.

The Elephant & Castle
Peckforton.

67

DROPPINGSTONE WELL, BICKERTON HILL, c.1905

This well, high on Bickerton Hill, near Raw Head, can still be found beside the Sandstone Trail long distance footpath. The people in this postcard appear to be carefully posed for the photographer, and include a well-dressed gentleman in a trilby hat, and a farm worker collecting water using a yoke to carry his buckets. Wells such as this one were often the only supply of water for local farms and houses. Nearby a precariously balanced rock overhanging a cliff is called 'The Droppingstone' and gives this well its name.

Old Copper Mine, Bickerton Hill   J.V.B.

THE COPPER MINES, BICKERTON HILL, 1907
Copper mining at Bickerton has a long history. In 1697 the landowner Sir Philip Egerton of Oulton
Park employed a German engineer, Herr Brandshagen, to survey the area. He found at least five
mineshafts already operating under harsh conditions. Samples of the ore revealed a rich copper
content and he agreed to re-organise the operations. Mining continued until the nineteenth century.
This engine-house was built in 1856, but the mines closed shortly afterwards, as the ore seams
were not very productive. The mine buildings have now disappeared, but the chimney can still
be seen near Gallantry Bank.

BARNHILL SMITHY, BROXTON, 1912

This group of buildings can be found near the Durham Heifer inn, at the top of the hill from Broxton on the road to Nantwich. In front of the smithy doors are the two blacksmiths in their aprons. The building is still standing, although disused. The house on the right also served as a post office for the hamlet; behind it the thatched cottage was rebuilt in 1931. Two interesting local industries, now defunct, were the making of besom brooms from heather and birch twigs and the quarrying of silver sand, which was used as a scouring powder and for spreading on cottage floors.

pp 80 - 81

Pictures are on pages opposite to related captions!

BARNHILL SMITHY, Broxton.   J.V.B.

HARTHILL VILLAGE, 1905

Nestling beneath the tree-covered hills and cliffs of Bickerton and Burwardesley, the village has a picturesque situation. It was essentially an estate village for the Bolesworth Estate, which built these unusual cottages around the green in 1844. In the surrounding hills are caves, which, according to local legend, were inhabited by thieves. In 1834 the daughter of the vicar of Tattenhall wrote in her diary about the dreadful brigands of Bloody Bones Cave, on Raw Head, who terrorised the neighbourhood, plundering graves and stealing cheeses from farms.

A Merry Christmas and a Happy New Year.

CHURCH BANK, TATTENHALL.
PERFECTION SERIES 1895.

CHURCH BANK, TATTENHALL, 1905

Tattenhall, eight miles south east of Chester, has origins dating back to Roman times. In the centre of the village, Church Bank leads off the High Street and is where John Wesley preached on his visits in the 1760s. The trees and cobbled road surface have now gone, but the buildings remain, though altered. The shop has been converted to a house called Tudor Cottage and dates from the seventeenth century, whilst the building behind the trees is now a bank. The billboards proclaim the death of Sir Henry Irving and date the photograph to shortly after the 13 October 1905. Note how this postcard has been overprinted for use as a Christmas card.

THE BOYS' HOME, TATTENHALL, 1906

This early-nineteenth-century building in the centre of Tattenhall is now known as Olympus House and is used as offices. It was originally a private school, but around 1895 it was taken over by the Church of England as a home for 'waifs and strays'. This postcard shows some of the boys with their band outside the home. They attended local schools and at one time there was concern about the extent to which corporal punishment was used on the boys. The home closed in 1939 and was used during the war for billeting soldiers.

LADIES' CLUB PROCESSION, TATTENHALL, c.1908

Tattenhall Wakes Week was held in the last week of June. On the Monday the Ladies' Club, who were members of the Female Friendly Society, marched in procession through the village, headed by a brass band, often that of the Cheshire Militia. The Ladies' Club were held in high esteem locally and were said 'to do much good'. Here a large crowd is watching the procession. Included are children from the Boys' Home, seen behind railings on the left, all wearing suits and cloth caps.

HANDLEY CHESHIRE
PERFECTION SERIES 1405.

HANDLEY VILLAGE, 1907

Handley, meaning 'high pasture', stands above the plain of the Dee valley on the Chester to Whitchurch road. This postcard view looks south from the church. The black and white cottage, one of several in the village, dates from 1601, but has had its thatched roof replaced by tiles. In the background is the Calveley Arms, a coaching inn. There were originally three other inns in Handley to serve travellers.

ALDFORD VILLAGE, c.1905

This village, between Chester and Farndon, has a long history, including a castle built in the twelfth century. However it was transformed into a 'model village' by its owners, the Grosvenor Estate, in the 1860s. The cottages were designed by the architect John Douglas and incorporated details such as barley twist chimney stacks and patterned brickwork. Each cottage was given a large garden and accommodation for a cow, pigs and hens. The estate also provided a shop, pub and church. The village still retains the atmosphere of self-sufficiency, although most of the inhabitants now work elsewhere.

CHURTON VILLAGE, NEAR FARNDON.

"The Unique Series".

CHURTON, NEAR FARNDON, 1910

A view of the centre of Churton, looking towards Farndon, with Pump Lane on the left. The half-timbered, thatched building on the right is The Old Red Lion public house. It was severely damaged by fire in the 1930s and was subsequently rebuilt as a house. Outside, note the covered wagon, probably that of a travelling salesman with a queue of customers. Like its neighbour, Aldford, Churton has close connections with the Grosvenor Estate. The population of the village increased rapidly in the nineteenth century, as workers were required for the rebuilding of Eaton Hall.

THE BRIDGE, FARNDON.   "The Unique Series".

FARNDON BRIDGE, 1907

Farndon and its Welsh neighbour, Holt, grew around this important crossing of the River Dee. The bridge, though much modified, dates from 1345 and has nine arches with pointed buttresses and cut-waters. There was originally a gatehouse at the Welsh end, but this has now gone. Two sons of the Welsh prince Madoc were thrown over the parapet and drowned by their guardians in order to gain an inheritance. It is said that their screams can still be heard on dark nights, and their ghosts haunt the arches. A new bridge now carries the traffic to Wales and this scene has regained its former tranquillity.

THE HIGH STREET, FARNDON, 1905

Farndon suffered badly during the Civil War, from 1643-45. Many of the buildings were destroyed and the church was badly damaged. Most of the village was rebuilt after this date. In this view of the High Street the Nags Head Inn can be seen on the extreme left. The shops and cottages next to it have now been rebuilt. Across the road is the Raven Hotel, from which the Great Western Railway ran a pioneering bus service to Wrexham in the early 1900s. Behind is the Congregational Church, now replaced by an ugly modern building. The district was noted for its strawberries, as discovered by the sender of this postcard, who was on holiday in the village and writes, 'At the house where we we are staying we have strawberries for every meal.'

BARTON ROAD, FARNDON.   "The Unique Series".

BARTON ROAD, FARNDON, 1907

This fine row of thatched half-timbered cottages is typical of south Cheshire. Unfortunately Pinnington's grocers shop, on the left, has now been replaced by a red brick building. The rest of the terrace can still be seen, though enlarged to include dormer windows. Notice the cap and apron worn by the woman outside the well stocked shop. Nearby is the village lock-up or gaol, dated 1837 and now in use as a garage.

Cock O' Barton. Cheshire. 1904.

THE COCK O'BARTON, NEAR FARNDON, 1904

A waggoner and his team of two horses stop for refreshment at the Cock Inn at Barton. The village is on the old salt route from Nantwich to Wales, and was known for cock fighting and bear baiting. The inn was built around 1800, by the Carden Estate, to serve the coaching trade. Note the cycles parked outside. The Edwardian period saw a great increase in cycling for recreation. Cycle touring holidays were especially popular and many country pubs advertised 'accommodation for cyclists'.

South Front, Carden Hall, Cheshire.   Willett's Series.

CARDEN HALL, CLUTTON, 1909

Carden Park, south of the village of Clutton, was the home of the Leche family from the fourteenth century, when John Leche was surgeon to Edward III. The house shown on this postcard was built in the sixteenth century and was noted for its fine half-timbering. On the night of 16 September 1912, fire broke out in the gentlemen's smoking room and quickly spread to the rest of the building, which was destroyed. The occupants escaped unharmed, but valuable jewellery and antiques were lost. Only the stables and two lodges remain. There are now plans to use the park as a country pursuits centre.

THE GREEN, TILSTON, NEAR MALPAS, c.1915

The village of Tilston dates back to Saxon times. This view of the green, looking towards Stretton, shows two of the four inns which once served the village. On the left is the Carden Arms, and the Fox and Hounds is at the end of the row of buildings to the right. In the foreground is the village smithy, with an interesting assortment of farm implements outside. This and the adjoining thatched cottage have been demolished and their site is now a car park for the Fox and Hounds.

The Cross, Malpas.

Published by CHEERS & HOPLEY, Photographic Chemists.

THE CROSS, MALPAS, 1905

This quaint little town, well away from main roads, was one of the most powerful English baronies in the reign of Henry I, and possessed a castle which has now completely disappeared. The square leading up to the church steps is shown here. Cheers and Hopley, publishers of this postcard, owned the shop in the centre of the picture. It incorporated a chemist and shaving rooms. To its left was the New Inn, later converted to a grocer's shop, and the Crown Hotel is at the end of the row. A London and North Western Railway notice board can be seen on its wall. The cross dominating the scene is relatively modern; it was built in 1877, in memory of Mr Thurlow, a former rector.

OLDHALL STREET, MALPAS, CHESHIRE.

T.S.
B.&C.

"The Unique Series.'

OLDHALL STREET, MALPAS, 1905

Oldhall Street derives its name from the old residence of the Brereton family, which used to be situated at its southern end before it burnt down in 1760. The Red Lion Inn can be seen at the top of the street, on the right. It was visited by James I in 1624, and the chair used by the King is still said to be there. The building, however, was rebuilt in 1920. The half-timbered house nearest the camera has been demolished, but the cottages to its left are now restored and were given a conservation award in 1991.

Cholmondeley Castle, Malpas, Cheshire.

CHOLMONDELEY CASTLE, c.1904

The Cholmondeley family have lived here for over eight hundred years, deriving their name from Calmunds Lea, the original place name. Until 1804 their house occupied the same site. It was rebuilt in 1571 and was the centre of a battle, in 1643, during the Civil War. In 1801 the present castle was started some distance from the old building. It took three years to build, and the Marquess of Cholmondeley designed parts of it himself. During the work the cottages of the old village were demolished to make way for the gardens and were rebuilt at the edge of the park. Only a fragment of the earlier house now remains, but the chapel, dating back to 1285, can still be seen in the grounds.

Cheshire Yeomanry Band, Cholmondeley, 1910

THE CHESHIRE YEOMANRY BAND AT CHOLMONDELEY, 14 May 1910
In May 1910 the Cheshire Yeomanry camped in Cholmondeley Park for their two weeks annual training. In all, 438 men and 23 officers took part. Due to heavy rain the park rapidly became a quagmire, and it was reported in the press that even the Duke of Westminster, who had recently joined the regiment, was seen using a spade to dig himself out of his tent. This postcard of the Yeomanry Band is taken in the yard of Castle Farm. When the present castle and park were built, in 1804, an inn was moved to this site. Later it was converted to a farmhouse, shop and post office.
Mr and Mrs Dodd, who ran the shop, are seen seated with the band.

† VZPOMÍNÁME †

68.

CHOLMONDELEY PARK CAMP – 1. ZÁŘÍ 1940

'IN COMMEMORATION', CHOLMONDELEY PARK CAMP, 1 September 1940
Cholmondeley Park retained its military associations during World War II. In 1940, after Dunkirk,
Czech troops and airmen were billeted in the park for six months and were the subject of great
local interest. They were visited by President Benes and the Foreign Minister, Jan Masaryk of
the Czech government-in-exile. A memorial stone, which can still be seen in the park, was carved
by the sculptor Frank Belski, then a young soldier aged 18. This commemorative postcard was
probably issued when the troops were transferred away from the camp in September 1940.

WRENBURY VILLAGE, 1906

Looking along the village street towards the green and St Margaret's church, the wagon is passing where the village stores now stand. The building on the left, with the unusual half-timbering, is Stanley House, built in the 1860s. The land in front of it has now been developed for housing, and across the road the cottages on the right have been rebuilt. Wrenbury is mentioned in the Domesday Book, and at one time much of the village was owned by the monks of Combermere Abbey. It remained an isolated community until the building of the canal and the Whitchurch to Nantwich railway in the nineteenth century. Since World War II the village has doubled in size, but still retains its character.

CANAL AND DRAWBRIDGE, WRENBURY.

LLANGOLLEN CANAL AND DRAWBRIDGE, WRENBURY, 1908

The Ellesmere and Chester Canal, now known as the Llangollen Canal, was completed in 1796 and linked villages such as Wrenbury to the rest of the country, encouraging local industries. The commercial centre of Wrenbury is shown here. On the left is the canal warehouse, used for the despatch of cheese and dairy products. It is now the base of a pleasurecraft company. To the right is a Victorian water mill, one of two in the village, and now converted into a public house, 'The Dusty Miller'. The distinctive wooden lift-bridge is a feature of this canal.

South Cheshire Hounds.   Meet at Audlem, 12th March, 1907.

Arnold, Photo., Market Drayton.   Copyright.

MARKET SQUARE, AUDLEM, 1907

The fourteenth-century parish church of St James The Great dominates this view of the square at Audlem. In front of the church is the old butter cross, next to which is a bear stone, to which the animals were tethered for baiting during the local Wakes. The ornamental lamp was erected in 1877 as a memorial to Richard Bellyse, a local surgeon. On the left is a large advertisement on the end wall of the general stores. Cheese colouring, ale, stout and cattle medicine are some of the items mentioned. The date of the meet is interesting, as from 1907 the South Cheshire Hounds amalgamated with the North Cheshires to cover the whole county.

AUDLEM WHARF, c.1904

It is said that the hardest way to leave Cheshire is by canal at Audlem. Here Thomas Telford built a flight of fifteen locks on the Shropshire Union Canal in 1828. Commercial traffic was still important when this photograph of lock no.13 and the wharf was taken. The carts are collecting roadstone brought to Audlem by narrowboat. Pleasurecraft are now the main traffic on the canal, and the shed and crane have been removed. The wharfmans house on the right was converted to a pub, 'The Shroppie Fly', in the 1970s.

DODDINGTON HALL.

DODDINGTON HALL, 1908

Doddington Park, between Nantwich and Woore, was the home of the Delves family for many centuries. The tower of the original castle of 1364 still stands in the park. By the eighteenth century Doddington had passed to the Delves-Broughton family, and this hall was built by Samuel Wyatt between 1777 and 1798 in English Renaissance style. The entrance steps are thought to be by Adam, and the gardens were landscaped by Capability Brown. Until recently the hall was used as a girls' boarding school.

THE VILLAGE, BARTHOMLEY.

DAIRYMEN, FARM NEAR CREWE, 1906

This interesting postcard, although uncaptioned, is believed to have been photographed at a farm near Crewe. It shows a group of six farmworkers, equipped for milking, in the days before automation. Note the typical three-legged stools, pails and the yoke carried by the man on the right. Today, using modern machinery, the work of milking can be carried out by one person.

94

BARTHOMLEY VILLAGE, NEAR CREWE, 1912

Barthomley lies in the south-eastern corner of Cheshire, close to the Staffordshire border. This view is taken from the church, and shows several of the timber-framed cottages for which the village is noted. On the extreme right is the White Lion inn, which dates from 1614. The bridge over the Wulvarn Brook is in the centre of the picture. It derives its name from the last wolf in Britain, reputedly killed in the area. The parish church of St Bertoline was the scene of a massacre in 1643, during the Civil War, when twelve villagers, who had taken refuge in the tower, were killed by a troop of Royalist soldiers.

Communications to J. S. BREEZE, 34 Trafalgar Road, Birkdale.

THE LANCASHIRE AND CHESHIRE BIBLE VAN, c.1906

Surprisingly, the early years of the twentieth century were a period of falling church attendance and a drift away from religion. To combat this there were evangelist campaigns, such as the Great Welsh Revival in 1904-05, led by Evan Roberts. The evangelists used bible carriages, like this one, to tour villages, where prayer meetings would be held and religious literature sold. This carriage advertised, 'Good works old and new' and, 'Bibles sold here from 6d', in addition to the rather stern warnings painted on its side.

CHESHIRE POSTCARD PUBLISHERS

Local publishers who worked in the area covered by this book. Page numbers are given where an example is included.

A.E. Adams, Bunbury (59, 87)
C.E. Ardern, Lymm (2)
Aston, Tattenhall
Arnold, Market Drayton (91)
Berry, Nantwich
J.A. Bratt, Duddon (29)
C. Butler, Altrincham (9)
Mark Cook, Chester (74)
J.H. Crosse (The Eddisbury Series), Frodsham (22)
J.R. Crosse, Whitchurch (86)
Cheers & Hopley, Chester, Malpas, Saltney, Buckley (84)
Finlay Cumming, Tarporley
H. Davis, Northwich (11, 12, 16, 17)
Thos. Dutton, Winsford (65)
Llew Evans, Northwich (10, 18, 19, 49)
C.C.H. The Heather Series, Winsford (50)
F. Harold Haines, Tarporley (23, 25, 27, 28, 30-32, 34, 37, 44, 46-48, 53-55, 57, 61, 63, 64, 66, 67)
Johnson, Nantwich (89)
Jeffs Printers, Tarporley
Hugo Lang, Chester & Liverpool (45)
B.H. Lawie, Beeston Brook
T. Marshall, Winsford (52)
The Perfection Series (72, 73, 76, 92)
H.S. Purcell, Audlem
Rowlands, Tattenhall (95)
Shaw, Burslem (90, 93, 94)
Thos. Swift (The Unique Series), Chester (7, 14, 15, 24, 77-80, 85)
H.E. Tonge, Latchford (8)
J.V., Broxton (68-71)
S. Vernon, Tarporley (38)
S. Ward, Acton Bridge (5, 6)
Willett, Farndon (81, 82)

ACKNOWLEDGEMENTS

The author would like to thank the following for their invaluable help:

J. Salmon Ltd., Sevenoaks for their kind permission to reproduce the postcard used for the front cover.
Captain Gordon Fergusson
The staff of Chester Local History Library
The staff of Chester Record Office
Steve Benz; marketing and publishing
Frank Rhodes; editing and proof-reading

BIBLIOGRAPHY

O. Bott and R. Williams (1975) *Man's Imprint on Cheshire*
Cheshire W.I. (1952 & 1961) *Cheshire Village Memories Vols. I and II*
Cheshire W.I. (1990) *The Cheshire Village Book*
T.A. Coward (1904) *Picturesque Cheshire*
F. Crossley (1949) *Cheshire*
P. De Figueiredo and J. Treuherz *Cheshire Country Houses*
J. McN. Dodgson *The Place Names of Cheshire*
B. Jeuda (1987) *Railway Postcards of Cheshire*
Local History Group (1989) *Reflections of Old Tarvin*
N. Pevsner and E. Hubbard (1978) *The Buildings of England; Cheshire*
Edited by F.A. Latham *Cheshire Village Histories:* Tarporley (1973)
                        Cheshire Village Histories: Tattenhall (1977)
                        Cheshire Village Histories: Bunbury (1989)